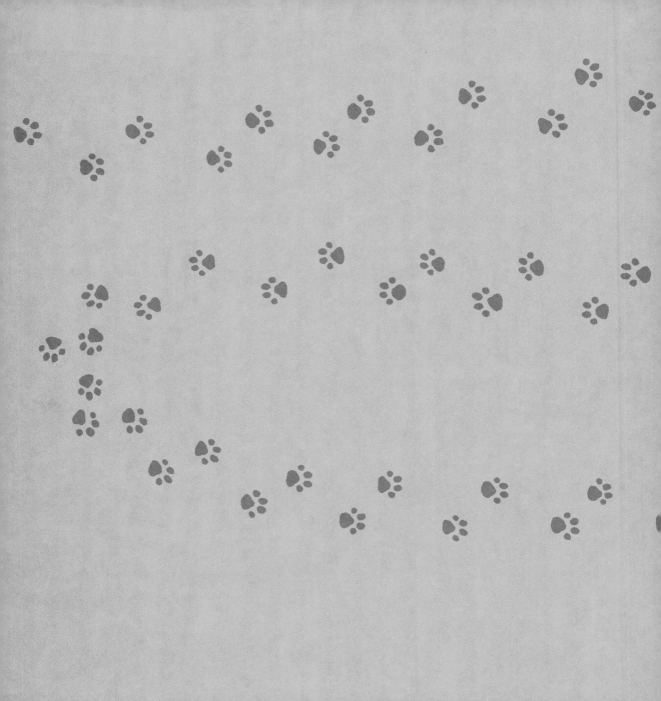

LET'S TALK ABOUT

ACCEPTING NO

by Joy Berry • Illustrated by Maggie Smith

SCHOLASTIC INC.

New York   Toronto   London   Auckland   Sydney
Mexico City   New Delhi   Hong Kong   Buenos Aires

ISBN 0-439-34155-8

10 9 8 7 6 5 4 3 2 1   02 03 04 05 06
Printed in the U.S.A.
First printing, February 2002

Hello, my name is Molly.

I live with Pia.

Sometimes Pia doesn't like it when
people tell her no.

Like Pia, you might not like it when people tell you no.

When someone tells you no, you might feel frustrated, angry, or disappointed.

You might even feel sorry for yourself.

There are lots of good reasons why someone might say no.

Someone might say no because you ask for something that might hurt you or another person.

Someone might say no because you
ask for something that isn't allowed.

Someone might say no because
you aren't being fair.

Someone might say no because the person
is busy when you ask for something.

Someone might say no because you ask
for something in a rude or bossy way.

If you don't want to be told no, ask for things that aren't against the rules or dangerous.

Only ask for your fair share.

And try to be considerate of other people when you ask for things.

When you ask for something, try to
do it in a calm and polite way.

Try not to get upset when someone tells you no.

Instead, try to find out why someone has told you no.

Sometimes you might feel frustrated or angry even though you understand why someone has told you no.

When this happens, try not to beg or whine.

Begging and whining won't help you get your way.

Try to accept it when someone tells you no.

Instead, ask to do something that you know someone will let you do.

When you get no for an answer,
try not to think about it too much.

Instead, think of something fun
that's okay for you to do.

Then do it!

It can be hard to accept no for an answer.

But cooperating when someone tells you no
is best for everyone.

Let's talk about . . . **Joy Berry!**

As the inventor of self-help books for kids, Joy Berry has written over 250 books that teach children about taking responsibility for themselves and their actions. With sales of over 80 million copies, Joy's books have helped millions of parents and their kids.

Through interesting stories that kids can relate to, Joy Berry's Let's Talk About books explain how to handle even the toughest situations and emotions. Written in a clear, simple style and illustrated with bright, humorous pictures, the Let's Talk About books are fun, informative, and they really work!

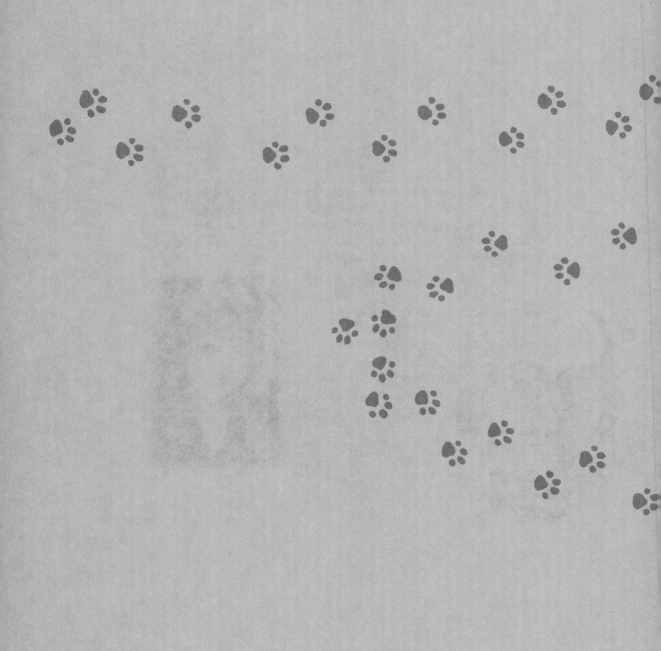